THE BIG COMFY COUCH ™

It's Mine!

Written by **Cheryl Wagner**

Illustrated by **Cheryl Roberts**

TIME LIFE Kids ™

ALEXANDRIA,
VIRGINIA

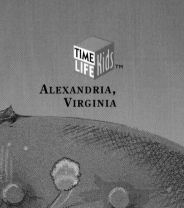

Loonette and her doll Molly
were busy as ever on the
Big Comfy Couch.
Loonette was teaching
Molly how to play a
card game.

"Do you have any cards
with queens on them,
Molly?" Loonette asked. "Or
should I 'go fish'?"

Just then, they heard a sound outside.
Bells and whistles could mean only one thing!

"You're right, Molly," Loonette announced,
jumping down from the couch. "Major
Bedhead IS coming. Let's go see what
he's bringing."

TO
LOONETTE
THE
CLOWN

Major Bedhead brought everyone's mail. Today he had a
special delivery to make.

"Package for Loonette the Clown. Package for Loonette
the Clown," he called.

"Oh, thank you," Loonette said excitedly. "I wonder
what it could be?"

Loonette quickly tore open the package. She pulled out six bright rings and a clown-shaped post.

"Look! It's a ringtoss game from my Auntie Macassar!" Loonette exclaimed. "This will be fun!"

Loonette went to work setting up the game. First she put the clown post on the ground. Then she took ten steps backward. She picked up the rings and began tossing them one by one.

It was fun trying to loop the rings around the clown. But it wasn't easy. It took practice.

Soon Major Bedhead wanted to take a turn.
"May I go next, please, Loonette?" he asked politely.
    But Loonette wasn't ready to share her new toy.
"No, it's still my turn, Major Bedhead," she replied.
"I just started playing."

Granny's cat, Snicklefritz, invented a new way to play the game. But Loonette didn't think it was such a great idea.

"Snicklefritz!" she cried. "Please don't get in the way! Can't you see this game is *mine*?"

Loonette didn't notice that her friends weren't having any fun at all.

Granny tried to help.

"Loonette, everyone would like to try your new game," she said gently. "Won't you share your toy with us?"

Loonette shook her head. She didn't feel like sharing.

"I have an idea," said Granny. "Why don't the rest of us keep busy by having a little picnic? While you enjoy your game, we'll enjoy some of my homemade chuckleberry tarts."

Loonette's friends had a delicious picnic. They shared lemonade and chuckleberry tarts and each other's company. Major Bedhead told his best joke. Everyone laughed and giggled.

Loonette kept looking at her friends. Her new toy didn't seem so important anymore.

"May I come to the picnic now?" Loonette asked finally. "I'm finished trying my ringtoss game."

"Of course. We'll share with you," Granny said, as she poured Loonette a glass of cool lemonade. "The more the merrier."

"Granny, what does it mean 'the more the merrier'?" Loonette asked.

"When you share with others, it's just more fun for everyone," Granny explained.

"That's true, Granny," said Loonette. She picked up the rings and announced, "And that gives me a great idea. Who wants a turn at my clown ringtoss game?"

Every clown, cat, and doll took a turn.
They all had a very merry time
sharing and playing together.